Lace
MAXI

Gerda Perik

FORTE PUBLISHERS

G000055312

Contents

© 2003 Forte Uitgevers, Utrecht
© 2003 for the translation by the publisher
Original title: *Lacé Maxi*

All rights reserved. No part of this publication may be copied, stored in an electronic file or made public, in any form or in any way whatsoever, either electronically, mechanically, by photocopying or any other form of recording, without the publisher's prior written permission.

Third printing November 2004
ISBN 90 5877 332 9

This is a publication from
Forte Publishers BV
P.O. Box 1394
3500 BJ Utrecht
The Netherlands

For more information about the creative books available from Forte Publishers:
www.forteuitgevers.nl

Publisher: Marianne Perlot
Editor: Hanny Vlaar
Photography and digital image editing:
Fotografie Gerhard Witteveen, Apeldoorn, the Netherlands
Cover and inner design:
BADE creatieve communicatie, Baarn, the Netherlands
Translation: TextCase Book Productions, Groningen, the Netherlands

Preface

This is my seventh Lacé book and I still enjoy working out new ideas. This time, there are six new Lacé templates. These templates are larger than the templates you have used in the past and I have, therefore, called them maxi-templates. You can use these templates to make various cards by using different grooves. Since there is more room on these templates, the grooves have been numbered. You can make pretty cards using the larger grooves, but the smaller grooves are also very nice to use. Use the scrap pieces of Lacé paper to make gift labels. It is a good idea to always have a large number of these at hand.

Crafters often ask me which book they should buy, the first or the latest? It doesn't really matter which book you buy, because each book includes different ideas.

Gerda

Thanks: Marianne Perlot for allowing me once again to write a book. Mariëlle, thank you for helping with the text. I also wish to thank Hanny Vlaar for proofreading my text.

Techniques

Lacé cutting

The pattern to be cut out is shown on the light green Lacé templates. Preferably use the attractive Lacé paper. Stick the template in the correct place on the card using non-permanent adhesive tape or napkin tape (do not tape it to the cutting mat). Use a Lacé knife or an Olfa knife to cut through the openings, starting at the point and cutting towards the side. Hold the knife vertical when cutting. Always use a knife with a sharp point.

The new maxi-templates, which are numbered 43 to 48, are larger than the older templates and there is, therefore, enough space to write the number of each groove on the template. The smallest shape on the Lacé template is always groove no. 1.

The long side of each template is marked with centimetre marks.

You can make various different cards using only one Lacé template. For each card, I have indicated which grooves I have used.

After cutting, carefully remove the template from the card. It is important to first score the borders which are going to the folded using the Lacé scoring and folding tool. Next, fold the scored borders over. You can either leave them as they are or stick them down using double-sided adhesive tape. Not sticking down the borders gives a playful effect.

Tip

Do not remove the knife from the card or the template when cutting along the grooves. For the templates with circular grooves, it is easier if you rotate the card. Tape the template to the card and then tape the card to the cutting mat. You can then turn the cutting mat so that you can cut along the curve in a flowing movement. Remember to keep the knife vertical, though, because only then will you be able to cut right into the corners of the grooves.

Left and right-handed people

It is easier for right-handed people to cut the template with the word Lacé at the top. For left-handed people, it is easier if the word Lacé is at the bottom.

Eyelets

Apart from the usual eyelets, there are now also mini-eyelets. They are also available as flowers, hearts, leaves, hands, etc. Instructions: use the punch and a hammer to make a hole in the correct place on the card. Place the card on a hard surface (an old cutting mat or a piece of

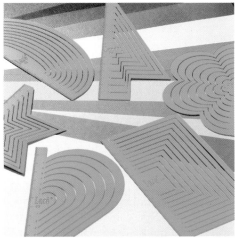

1. The Lacé paper used plus the six maxi-templates.

2. Stick the template to the card.

3. By using different grooves, you can make different cards with the same template.

4. Decorate the card with a 3D picture.

wood). Push an eyelet or, for example, a flower and an eyelet into the hole. Turn the card over, place the striking tool in the eyelet and hit it with a hammer. The eyelet will then bend open. To avoid damaging the card, place a piece of paper or a piece of cloth under the eyelet when hitting it with the hammer.

Decorative stones

Decorative stones can be purchased in attractive colours. They are also available as self-adhesive stones. Still use a small amount of glue to stick them to the card, to prevent them from falling off when the card is placed in or taken out of the envelope.

3D cutting

A cutting pattern is given for some pictures. Carry out the following if you use other pictures: cut the entire picture out first and stick it on the card using glue, 3D glue or foam tape. For the second layer, do not cut out what is in the background. For the third layer, only cut out what is in the foreground. Slightly bend the second and third layers and use 3D glue or foam tape to stick them on top of the first picture. If you use 3D glue, leave it to dry for a little while.

For the very small pictures, only stick one layer on the card using 3D glue or foam tape, bending the pictures slightly.

Mouse cutting patterns

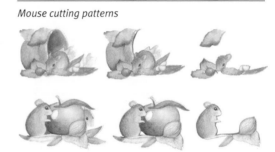

Cutting patterns for the cards on the cover

Materials

- ❏ Card: Artoz (A) and Canson Mi-Teintes (C)
- ❏ Different colours of Lacé paper
- ❏ Lacé templates no. 43 to 48.
- ❏ Lacé knife or Olfa knife
- ❏ Lacé ruler
- ❏ Lacé scorer and folding tool

- ❏ Lacé cutting mat
- ❏ Eyelets and eyelet shapes in various colours
- ❏ Eyelets toolkit
- ❏ Corner and figure punches
- ❏ Corner ornament punches
- ❏ Border ornament punches
- ❏ Hand punches (Fiskars)

- ❏ Cutting sheets: Marianne Design, Eline Pellinkhof, Marjoleine Zweed, Picturel and Shake-it
- ❏ Border stickers, decorative stickers and text stickers
- ❏ Identi-pen
- ❏ Ribbons

Cards on the cover

Autumn bouquet with blackberries
Lacé paper: mother-of-pearl blue/white • Card: bright yellow (C400) – double card (14.8 x 10.5 cm) • Eyelets: yellow flowers and blue eyelets • Cutting sheet 3D 407 • Blue gel pen • Lacé template no. 44 (grooves 7 and 6)

Cut the grooves in the blue Lacé paper (14.8 x 10 cm). Cut the paper through the middle. Attach the blue paper to the yellow card using eyelets. Decorate with a 3D picture and draw a decorative line using a blue gel pen.

Autumn bouquet with blue hydrangeas
Lacé paper: mother-of-pearl blue/white • Card: bright yellow (C400) • Decorative stickers: corners and lines

• Cutting sheet 3D 407 • Lacé template no. 44 (grooves 8 and 6)

Make a blue double card (14 x 14 cm) and cut the pattern out of it. Make a yellow *flower* for the middle using groove 5. Stick a yellow square (14 x 14 cm) against the inside on the left-hand side. Decorate with a 3D picture and some corner stickers. Stick a line sticker around the *flower*.

Cards on page 1 and page 3
These small cards are made from scrap pieces of Lacé paper and pictures. Use the small grooves to cut the pattern out. Make these cards for flower bouquets and gifts.

Mice

All these cards are made using cutting sheet 3D 407.

1. Mouse with hazelnuts

Lacé paper: mother-of-pearl blue/white – blue double card (12.5 x 12.5 cm) • Line sticker • Blue gel pen • Lacé template no. 44 (grooves 7 and 6)
Cut the pattern out of the right-hand side as far as the middle of the card. Cut off the right-hand side. Decorate the card with a line sticker and a 3D picture.

2. Mouse with an apple

Lacé paper: mother-of-pearl blue/white – blue/white double card (14.8 x 10.5 cm) • Card: bright yellow (C400) • Double corner punch (bow) • Yellow stamp-pad ink • Lacé template no. 44 (grooves 5 and 2)
Cut out two rectangles: one yellow (14.5 x 10 cm) and one blue (2 mm smaller). Punch out the corners of the smallest rectangle. Cut half of the *flower* out of the blue one. Dab the yellow stamp-pad ink around the border. Stick everything on the card and add a 3D picture.

3. Mouse and a mushroom

Lacé paper: mother-of-pearl blue/white – blue/white double card (14 x 14 cm) • Card: bright yellow (C 400) • Blue mini-eyelets • Photo corner figure punch • Lacé template no. 44 (grooves 7, 6, 5 and 4)
Make two squares: one yellow (13 x 13 cm) and one blue/white (12 x 12 cm). Cut the pattern out of the smallest square. Punch out the corners of the yellow square and slide the square with the pattern cut out of it in the corners. Attach everything to the double card using mini-eyelets. Stick the picture in the middle and make it 3D.

Cards 4 and 5 *(See the description given for the cards on the cover (page 7).*

6. Mouse and a flower pot

Lacé paper: mother-of-pearl blue/white – blue ouble card (14.8 x 10.5 cm) • Card: bright yellow (C400) • Brown stamp-pad ink • Lacé template no. 44 (grooves 5 and 4)
Cut a *flower* out of the middle of the blue card using groove 5. Place the template in the mirror image of the previous position and cut out the entire flower. Repeat this for the yellow card (14.7 x 10.3 cm) using groove 4 and stick this inside the double card. Punch out the corners of a white rectangle (24.8 x 10.5 cm) and make a 0.5 cm wide frame for the card. Stick the 3D picture in the middle.

Babies

Decorate these cards using, for example, decorative stickers and 3D pictures.

1. Baby things

Lacé paper: mother-of-pearl blue/white • Card: salmon (C384) – double card (13.5 x 13.5 cm) • Marjoleine background sheet (1181) • Picturel cutting sheet (1011) • Lacé template no. 46 (grooves 10, 9, 7 and 6)

Make two squares: one from the background paper (13 x 13 cm) and one from the blue paper (0.5 cm smaller). Cut the pattern out of the left-hand side of the blue square. Stick background paper (7 x 7 cm) in the middle.

2. Baby in a basket

Lacé paper: old rose/white – old rose double card (14.8 x 10.5 cm) • Marjoleine background paper (1181) • Border sticker • Cutting sheet AK019 • Lacé template no. 43 (grooves 9, 8, 7 and 6)

Cut the pattern out of the right-hand side and cut the rest of the right-hand side off. Stick background paper (14.8 x 10.5 cm) on the left-hand side.

3. Rusk with aniseed comfits

Lacé paper: mother-of-pearl blue/white – blue double card (13.5 x 13.5 cm) • Marjoleine background paper (1181) • Cutting sheet 3D 356 • Mini-eyelets: hands and eyelets • Border sticker • Lacé template no. 46 (grooves 9 and 4)

Make two squares: one from the background paper (13 x 13 cm) and one from the blue/white Lacé paper (0.5 cm smaller). Place the template at the top of the white square. Cut out the pattern and fold the border forwards. Use the eyelets to keep the different layers in place.

4. Baby coat

Lacé paper: old rose/white – old rose double card (13.5 x 13.5 cm) • Background paper (AK021) • Border sticker • Cutting sheet 3D 356 • Lacé template no. 45 (grooves 7 and 6)

Cut the pattern out of the left-hand side. Cut the heart out of the background paper using groove 5. Stick background paper (13.5 x 13.5 cm) on the left-hand side. Stick the pictures around the heart using 3D glue.

5. Doll's pram

Lacé paper: mother-of-pearl blue/white – blue double card (14.8 x 10.5 cm) • Marjoleine background paper (1178) • Picturel cutting sheet (1011) • Mini-eyelets: blue bows and yellow eyelets • Lacé template no. 43 (grooves 8 and 6)

Cut out two rectangles: one from the background paper (14 x 10 cm) and one from the blue/white Lacé paper (0.5 cm smaller). Cut the pattern out of the right-hand side of the smallest rectangle and cut the rest of the right-hand side off. Stick the layers together using the mini-eyelets.

6. Hurray, a girl

Lacé paper: old rose/white – old rose double card (13.5 x 13.5 cm) • Marjoleine background paper (1182) • Border stickers • Cutting sheet (Af019) • Corner ornament punch • Lacé template no. 45 (grooves 8, 7, 6 and 5)

Make two squares: one from the background paper (12.5 x 12.5 cm) and one from the rose paper (0.5 cm smaller). Punch out the corners of the background paper square. Cut the pattern out of the smallest square. Cut both the inside and the outside of the pattern off. Make the heart out of old rose paper using groove 4.

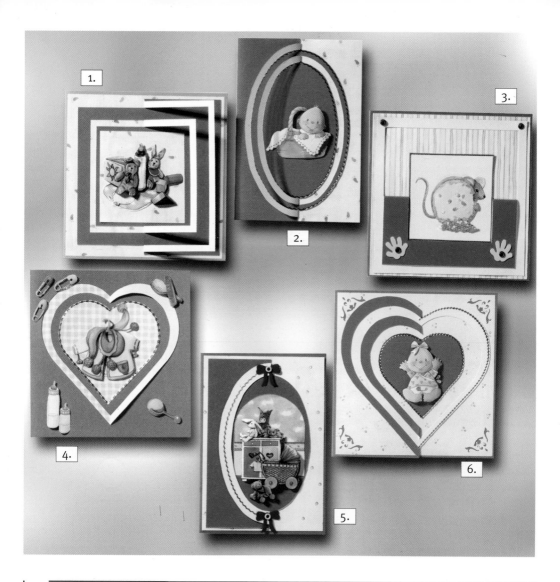

Marriage

Decorate these cards using decorative stickers and 3D pictures from the Picturel cutting sheet (1012).

1. Bridal bouquet
Lacé paper: old rose and pastel pink – old rose double card (13.5 x 13.5 cm) • Border stickers • Eyelets • Lacé template no. 45 (grooves 7 and 5)
Cut the pattern out of the right-hand side of a pastel pink square (13 x 13 cm). Punch eyelets in and around the heart.

2. The things needed for a wedding
Lacé paper: old rose • Card: white (A211) – double card (13.5 x 13.5 cm) • Eyelets and heart shapes • Line stickers • Lacé template no. 45 (grooves 8, 7, 6 and 5)
Cut the pattern out of the right-hand side of an old rose square (13 x 13 cm). Cut the pattern off around the outside of the template. Stick the square on the card using eyelets.

3. The bride's hat
Lacé paper: pastel pink • Card: white (A211) – double card (13.5 x 13.5 cm), wine red (A519) • Gold bradletz • Photo corner figure punch • Line sticker • Lacé template no. 45 (grooves 7 and 6)
Make two squares: one from wine red card (13 x 13 cm) and one from pastel pink card (12 x 12 cm). Punch out the corners of the wine red square. Cut the pattern out of the left-hand side of the pastel pink card and slide this square between the punched out corners of the wine red card. Attach bradletz in the punched out hearts.

4. Cheers
Lacé paper: old rose – double card (13.5 x 13.5 cm) • Marjoleine background paper • Border stickers • Lacé template no. 45 (grooves 8 and 6)
Make two squares: one from the background paper (13.2 x 13.2 cm) and one from the old rose paper (2 mm smaller). Cut the pattern out of the right-hand side of the smallest square and cut the rest of the right-hand side off. Cut out a white heart using groove 5.

5. Wedding cake
Lacé paper: old rose – double card (14.5 x 10.5 cm) • Line sticker • Border ornament punch • Lacé template no. 45 (grooves 6 and 5)
Cut the pattern out of the right-hand side of an old rose rectangle (14 x 10.3 cm). Punch a border of hearts in the middle of the top and bottom of the card.

Autumn

Decorate these cards using decorative stickers and 3D pictures from the cutting sheet 3D406.

1. Blue tits in love
Lacé paper: bronze/golden yellow and mother-of-pearl blue – bronze double card (14 x 14 cm) • Border stickers • Lacé template no. 46 (grooves 9 and 7)
Make two single cards: one blue (13.5 x 13.5 cm) and one bronze (0.5 cm smaller). Cut the pattern out of the right-hand side of the smallest square. Cut a square out of the middle using groove 3. Punch out the corners.

3. Great tits on a sunflower which has gone to seed
Lacé paper: bronze/golden yellow and a scrap piece of mother-of-pearl blue – bronze double card (13.5 x 13.5 cm) • Border stickers • Lacé template no. 46 (grooves 9, 8, 7 and 6)
Cut the pattern out of the left-hand side. Stick blue paper (13.5 x 13.5 cm) inside on the left-hand side.

2. Sparrow with a red berry
Lacé paper: bronze/golden yellow and mother-of-pearl blue – bronze double card (14.8 x 10.5 cm) • Line sticker • Lacé template no. 46 (grooves 7, 6, 5 and 4)
Cut the pattern out of the right-hand side and cut the rest of the right-hand side off. Stick a blue card (14.8 x 10.5 cm) on the left-hand side. Cut out a blue square (5 x 5 cm) and stick it in the middle.

4. Birds on a CD
Lacé paper: mother-of-pearl blue – blue double card (14.8 x 10.5 cm) • Card: salmon (C384) • CD • Border sticker • Lacé template no. 45 (grooves 6 and 5)

Cut the pattern out of the right-hand side and cut the rest of the right-hand side off.
Cut the heart out of the middle using groove 5. Stick the CD behind this heart. Stick a salmon card (14.8 x 10.5 cm) inside on the left-hand side.

5. Bird table

Lacé paper: mother-of-pearl blue – blue double card (14 x 14 cm) • Card: salmon (C384) • Border sticker • Lacé template no. 45 (grooves 7 and 6)
Make two squares: one salmon (13.5 x 13.5 cm) and one blue (2 mm smaller). Cut the pattern out of the smallest square. Cut out the entire heart using groove 6. Cut out a blue heart for the middle using groove 5.

6. Flower pot with great tits

Lacé paper: mother-of-pearl blue • Card: salmon (C384) – double card (13.5 x 13.5 cm) • White border sticker • Lacé template no. 45 (groove 7)
Cut the heart shape out upside down to make a spade. Only one groove is used. The right-hand side is folded inwards. Cut the spade out again from blue Lacé paper using groove 5 and stick it in the middle.

Pumpkins

All the cards are made using mother-of-pearl green/white Lacé paper. Decorate these cards using decorative stickers and 3D pictures from the cutting sheet 3D 408.

1. Get well soon

Romak text sheet • Line sticker • Lacé template no. 45 (grooves 8 and 6)

Make a double card (14 x 14 cm). Cut the pattern out of the right-hand side and cut the rest of the right-hand side off. Stick a piece of the text sheet (14 x 14 cm) inside on the left-hand side. Decorate the card with a line sticker which has been stuck on a 0.3 mm wide green border.

2. Watering can with flowers

Photo corner figure punch • Lacé template no. 44 (grooves 7, 6, 5 and 4)

Make a double card (13 x 13 cm). Cut the pattern out of the left-hand side. Make a square (12 x 12 cm), punch out the corners and cut it out to make a 0.5 cm wide border.

3. Washtub with a bouquet of flowers

Romak text sheet • Decorative stickers • Gold gel pen • Lacé template no. 44 (grooves 6, 5, 4 and 3)

Make a double card (14.8 x 10.5 cm). Cut the pattern out of the right-hand side and cut the rest of the right-hand side off. Cut the flower out of the middle using groove 3. Stick a piece of

the text sheet (14.8 x 10.5 cm) inside on the left-hand side.

4. Watering can and a sunflower
Romak text sheet • Decorative stickers • Line stickers • Lacé template no. 44 (groove 6)
Make a double card (14.8 x 10.5 cm). Cut the pattern out of the left-hand side. Stick a piece of the text sheet (14.7 x 10.4 cm) inside on the left-hand side.

5. Bucket and pumpkins
Photo corner figure punch • Lacé template no. 45 (grooves 5 and 3)

Make a double card (14.8 x 10.5 cm). Cut the pattern out of the left-hand side. Make a green rectangle (14.5 x 10 cm), punch out the corners and use it to make a 0.5 cm wide frame.

6. Basket with pumpkins
Romak text sheet • Line sticker • Lacé template no. 45 (grooves 8, 7, 6 and 5)
Make a double card (13.5 x 13.5 cm). Cut the pattern out of the right-hand side and cut the rest of the right-hand side off. Cut the heart out of the middle using groove 5. Make a square (13.5 x 13.5 cm) from the text sheet and stick it inside on the left-hand side.

Party

Decorate these cards using decorative stickers and 3D pictures from the Picturel cutting sheets (538, 1014 and 1015).

1. Fruit cake and a party hat

Lacé paper: mother-of-pearl green/white – green double card (13.5 x 13.5 cm) • Card: mango (A575) • Lacé template no. 46 (grooves 9, 8, 7 and 6)
Make two single cards: one mango (13.2 x 13.2 cm) and one green (2 mm smaller). Cut the pattern out.

2. Cheers

Lacé paper: mother-of-pearl old rose/white – old rose double card (13.5 x 13.5 cm) • Border sticker • Purple Identi-pen • Corner ornament punch • Lacé template no. 46 (grooves 10, 9, 8 and 7)
Cut the pattern out of the left-hand side of the rose card (13 x 13 cm). Make a white square (8 x 8 cm) and punch out the corners. Colour the border sticker using the purple Identi-pen.

3. Cherry pie

Lacé paper: mother-of-pearl green/white – white double card (13.5 x 13.5 cm) • Card: mango (A575) • Corner ornament punch • Lacé template no. 46 (grooves 9 and 6)
Cut the pattern out of the right-hand side and cut the rest of the right-hand side off. Make a mango card (13.5 x 13 cm) and stick it inside. Make two squares: one mango (7.8 x 7.8 cm) and one green (3 mm smaller). Punch out the corners.

4. Hurry, Merel is two years old

Lacé paper: old rose/white • Mini-eyelets: hands, cakes, balloons and bows • Lacé template no. 43 (grooves 9 and 6) • Old rose double card (15 x 10.5 cm)
Cut the pattern in the right-hand side and cut the rest of the right-hand side off. Fold the border over and punch eyelets in it to keep it in place.

5. A yummy cake

Lacé paper: mother-of-pearl green/white • Card: lobster red (A575) • Mini-eyelets • Lacé template no. 43 (grooves 7 and 4) • Green double card (13.5 x 13.5 cm)
Make two squares: one lobster red (13 x 13 cm) and one green (0.5 cm smaller). Cut the pattern in the left-hand side. Punch mini-eyelets in the border which has been folded over and in the corners.

6. Petits fours

Lacé paper: old rose/white • Marjoleine background paper • Lacé template no. 44 (grooves 8, 7, 6 and 5) • Old rose double card (13.5 x 13.5 cm)
Cut the pattern in the right-hand side and cut the rest of the right-hand side off. Stick background paper on the left-hand side. Cut a flower shape in the middle. Make an old rose square (13.5 x 13.5 cm) and stick it inside on the left-hand side.

Pink and white flowers

Decorate these cards using decorative stickers and 3D pictures.

1. White peony
Lacé paper: pastel green/white • Card: green (A309): double card (15 x 10.5 cm) • Eyelets: flowers • Line stickers • Shake-it cutting sheet (IT 384- Peony) • Lacé template no. 43 (grooves 9, 7, 4 and 3)
Cut the pattern out of the left-hand side and stick it down using flower eyelets. Make a rectangle (15 x 10.4 cm) from light green Lacé paper and stick it on the left-hand side.

2. Pink peony
Lacé paper: pastel pink/white: pastel pink double card (14.8 x 10.5 cm) • Card: wine red (A519) • Photo corner figure punch • Line sticker and sticker dots • Shake-it cutting sheet (IT 383- Peony) • Fiskars hand punch • Lacé template no. 43 (grooves 6 and 4)
Make two single cards: one wine red (14.5 x 10 cm) and one pastel pink (2 mm smaller). Cut the pattern out of the left-hand side of the smallest card. Cut an oval out of the middle using groove 3. Punch out wine red flowers and stick them in the corners.

3. Ovals with a pink peony
Lacé paper: pastel pink/white: pastel pink double card (16 x 11.5 cm) • Scrap piece of wine red card • Fiskars hand punch • Photo corner figure punch • Shake-it cutting sheet (IT 383) • Lacé template no. 43 (grooves 10, 9, 7, 6, 4 and 3)
Cut the pattern out of the right-hand side and cut the rest of the right-hand side off. Cut out a wine red oval for the middle using groove 3. Stick punched out flowers in the corners.

4. Marjoleine rose
Lacé paper: pastel pink/white: pastel pink double card (13 x 13 cm) • Card: wine red (A519) • Rounder c punch • Border sticker • Marjoleine cutting sheet (1119) • Lacé template no. 46 (grooves 10, 9, 8 and 7)
Cut the pattern out of the right-hand side. Cut a square out of the middle using groove 6. Make a wine red square (13 x 13 cm) and stick it on the left-hand side. Make a white square (7 x 7 cm) and punch out the corners.

5. Green photo frame
Lacé paper: pastel green/white: pastel green double card (13.5 x 13.5 cm) • Paper: dark green (A309) • Border ornament punch • Shake-it cutting sheet (IT 384) • Border sticker • Lacé template no. 43 (grooves 8, 7, 5 and 4)
Cut the pattern out of the right-hand side. Cut the oval out of the middle using groove 4.

Make a square (13.5 x 13.5 cm) from (thin) dark green paper. Stick it inside on the right-hand side and punch out the border. Also make a strip (14 x 2.5 cm) out of dark green paper and punch out a double border.

6. Pink rose between hearts

Lacé paper: pastel pink/white: pastel pink double card (13.5 x 13.5 cm) • Paper: wine red (A519) •

Border ornament punch • Eyelets and heart shapes • Marjoleine cutting sheet (1119) • Border sticker • Lacé template no. 46 (grooves 9 and 7)
Make two single cards: one wine red (13 x 13 cm) and one pastel pink (2 mm smaller). Cut the pattern out of the left-hand side of the smallest square. Make a square (8 x 8 cm) from (thin) wine red paper and punch out the borders.

Party cutting patterns

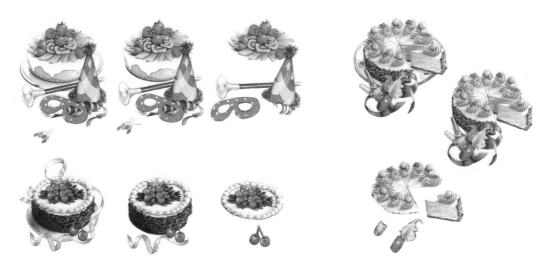

White Christmas

Stick all the layers on the card and punch eyelets in the corners. For all these cards, stick self-adhesive holographic paper inside on the left-hand side. Decorate these cards using decorative stickers and 3D pictures from the Picturel cutting sheets (500, 508 and 1009).

1. Candles

Card: white (A211): double card (13.5 x 13.5 cm) • Rainbow self-adhesive holographic paper • Eyelets and ice crystal shapes • Lacé template no. 48 (grooves 7, 6 and 5)
Cut the pattern out of the right-hand side and use the outside of the template to cut off the rest. Add eyelets. Stick white card inside on the left-hand side.

2. Window wreath

Card: white (A211): double card (13.5 x 13.5 cm) • Green self-adhesive holographic paper • Eyelets and star shapes • Green border stickers • Lacé template no. 48 (grooves 6 and 5)

Cut the pattern out of the right-hand side. Cut the tree out of the middle using groove 4. Add eyelets. Make a white inner card and cut the Christmas tree out of the middle of this card as well.

3. Merry Christmas and a Happy New Year

Card: white (A211): double card (13.5 x 13.5 cm) • Silver self-adhesive holographic paper • Silhouette cutting sheet (2205) • Red border sticker • Iris folding text sticker • Lacé template no. 48 (grooves 5 and 3)
Cut the pattern out of the left-hand side. Stick white card on the left-hand side.

4. Decorated Christmas branch

Card: white (A211): double card (13.5 x 13.5 cm) • Gold self-adhesive holographic paper • Fiskars star hand punch • Lacé template no. 47 (grooves 8, 7, 6 and 5)

Cut the pattern out of the right-hand side. Decorate by sticking a sheet of holographic paper (13.5 x 13.5 cm) and a white square on the left-hand side.

Stick blue holographic paper (13.5 x 13.5 cm) inside on the left-hand side. Cut the pattern out and cut the star out of the middle. Make a white square (13.5 x 13.5 cm) and stick it inside on the left-hand side. Stick the picture inside on the right-hand side, exactly behind the opening of the star.

5. Red star

Card: white (A211): double card (13.5 x 13.5 cm) • Red self-adhesive holographic paper • Red border stickers and line stickers • Fiskars hand punch • Red cord • Lacé template no. 47 (grooves 8 and 6) Cut the pattern out of the right-hand side and cut and use the outside of the template to cut off the rest. Punch two holes in the fold and thread a red cord through them.

6. Deer in the snow

Card: white card (A211): double card (13.5 x 13.5 cm) • Blue self-adhesive holographic paper • Fiskars star hand punch • Lacé template no. 47 (grooves 7 and 6 and groove 5 for the whole star)

Christmas trees

Decorate these cards using decorative stickers and 3D pictures from the mini 3D cutting sheets.

1. Lantern in a Christmas tree
Lacé paper: metallic mother-of-pearl dark blue/pastel blue: pastel blue double card (14.8 x 10.5 cm) • Corner silhouette punch • Gold gel pen • Star stickers • Lacé template no. 48 (grooves 6 and 3)
Cut the Christmas tree out of a scrap piece of Lacé paper. Place the template on the other half of the paper in a mirror image and cut out the other half of the Christmas tree. Also cut out the middle section.

2. Small candles in a Christmas tree
Lacé paper: metallic mother-of-pearl dark blue/pastel blue • Text vellum • Border stickers • Lacé template no. 48 (grooves 5 and 4) • Pastel blue double card (14.8 x 10.5 cm)
Cut the Christmas tree out of the right-hand side and use the outside of the template to cut off the rest. Stick the vellum inside on the left-hand side.

3. Blue tits in love
Lacé paper: metallic mother-of-pearl dark blue/pastel blue • Sticker stars and line stickers • Lacé template no. 48 (groove 6) • Dark blue double card (15 x 10.5 cm)
Make a square (14.5 x 9.8 cm) from Lacé paper and cut the Christmas tree out of it.

4. Snowman in a Christmas tree
Lacé paper: metallic mother-of-pearl malachite/pastel green • Line stickers and stars • Iris folding text sheet • Lacé template no. 48 (grooves 5 and 4) • Pastel green double card (13 x 13 cm)
Cut the pattern out of the left-hand side. Use groove 6 to cut off the rest of the right-hand side of the card.

5. Decorated birdhouse
Lacé paper: metallic mother-of-pearl malachite/pastel green: malachite double card (17 x 10.5 cm) • Text vellum • Border stickers and star stickers • Lacé template no. 48 (grooves 6 and 4)
Cut the pattern out of the right-hand side. Stick a piece of text vellum inside on the left-hand side.

6. Decorated Christmas tree
Lacé paper: metallic mother-of-pearl malachite/pastel green: malachite double card (15 x 10.5 cm) • Eyelets and ice crystal shapes • Lacé template no. 48 (grooves 7, 6, 5 and 4)
Cut the pattern out of the right-hand side and cut the rest of the right-hand side off. Add eyelets.

Christmas stars

Decorate these cards using decorative stickers and 3D pictures from the Picturel cutting sheets (533, 534 and 535).

1. Christmas bells

Lacé paper: metallic mother-of-pearl malachite/pastel green: malachite double card (14.8 x 10.5 cm) • Eyelets and stars shapes • Line stickers • Lacé template no. 47 (grooves 6 and 4)
Cut the pattern out of the right-hand side and fold the right-hand side inwards. Use eyelets to keep the points of the star in place.

2. Candles with Christmas decorations

Lacé paper: metallic mother-of-pearl malachite/pastel green: malachite double card (13 x 13 cm) • Text vellum • Star border sticker • Lacé template no. 47 (grooves 8 and 6)
Cut the pattern out of the right-hand side. Make a square (13 x 13 cm) from text vellum and stick it inside on the left-hand side.

3. Christmas decoration with holly and a candle

Lacé paper: metallic mother-of-pearl malachite/pastel green: double card (14.8 x 10.5 cm) • Star border sticker • Lacé template no. 47 (grooves 7 and 6)
Cut the pattern out of the right-hand side of the card and fold the rest inwards.

4. Christmas decoration with a medlar tree

Lacé paper: metallic mother-of-pearl dark blue/pastel blue • Text vellum • Lacé template no. 47 (grooves 6 and 5) • Malachite double card (13 x 13 cm).
Cut the pattern out of the right-hand side and use groove 8 to cut off the rest of the right-hand side. Make a square (13 x 13 cm) from text vellum and stick it inside the card on the left-hand side.

5. Holly

Lacé paper: metallic mother-of-pearl malachite/pastel green: double card (13.5 x 13.5 cm) • Border sticker • Double photo corner punch • Lacé template no. 47 (grooves 6 and 5)
Cut out a pastel green square (12.5 x 12.5 cm). Cut the pattern out of this square and cut out a star using groove 3. Punch out two corners.

6. Salmon-coloured Christmas decoration

Lacé paper: metallic mother-of-pearl dark blue/pastel blue: dark blue double card (13.5 x 13.5 cm) • Silver border sticker • Lacé template no. 47 (grooves 8 and 7)
Cut the pattern out of the right-hand side and cut the rest of the right-hand side off.

Many thanks to Kars and Co. for supplying the materials.

The materials used can be ordered by shopkeepers from: Kars & Co B.V. in Ochten, the Netherlands.